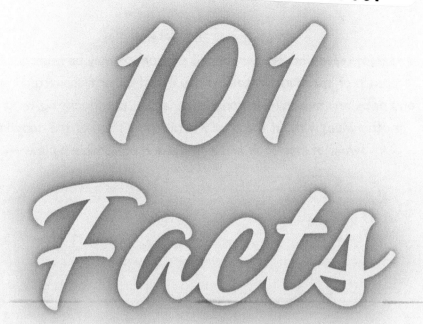

101 Facts

ABOUT TAYLOR SWIFT

QUIZZES, QUOTES, JOURNALS, AND MORE!

Table of contents

the First

Act

Welcome Swiftys!

We all love Taylor Swift. She started as a young girl with big dreams and an even bigger heart. From there she took on the world by storm and changed what we think of music today. She has been able to unite people from all different sorts of musical styles and create a cult-like following in each of them around the world. She did it with grace, love, and a whole lot of talent. But who is Taylor Swift and how did she become one of the most awarded and well-known stars we see today? I can't wait to share her stories with you, her quotes and get to know all things Taylor!

Fun Facts!

- Taylor Swift was born on December 13, 1989.
- Her parents named her Taylor because it was gender-neutral. They didn't want her to have a hard time getting a job because she was a girl.
- They also named her after their favorite singer James Taylor.
- Her mother's name is Andrea Finlay and her father is Scott Kingsley Swift.

A Star is Born

Taylor Swift was born in Reading, Pennsylvania to her mother Andrea, and her father Scott. They were both hard workers and loved their jobs. Her mother worked in marketing and her father worked with stocks and they were both very successful at it. She had a brother named Austin who was born when she was 2 years old. After he was born her mother stopped working to be home with them full-time. Her whole family was very close and loving from the beginning so she had a wonderful childhood. She often talks about her wonderful childhood experiences.

Fun Facts!

- Taylor Swift grew up on a Christmas tree farm.
- Her middle name is Allison after her aunt.
- She has blue-green eyes
- She loves riding horses and used to do it all the time as a kid.
- She loves animals and used to play with squirrels and bunnies at her farm and was able to make a lot of them her pets. She would sing to them and tell them stories

"I want to be defined by the things I love."
-Taylor swift

Create a collage or list of things you love. Use colorful pens, stickers, and drawings to personalize it. Think about the books, places, and things that define you.

Life at Christmas Tree farm

Taylor Swift often talks about her great memories while living with her grandma on the Christmas tree farm. She was alone a lot and left to play and ride horses. Her parents have said they never had to discipline her that much because she was always the first one to discipline herself. Her first experience with singing was with her grandma who was an opera singer and helped her foster her love of singing. She did regular things just like you did like chores and school. One of her jobs was rescuing the trees by picking out praying mantis. that were on them.

9

Fun Facts!

- As a child, Taylor Swift looked up to LeAnn Rimes, The Dixie Chicks, and Shania Twain as some of her favorite singers.
- Her grandmother, a former opera singer, was also a major influence in her love for music.
- One of the earliest people to teach Taylor about music was a computer repairman who taught her to play three guitar chords when she was 12 years old. This sparked her interest in music and inspired her to start writing songs. Her very first song was titled "Lucky You."

The Big Move

When Taylor was just a 5th-grader, she packed up her bags and moved to Wyomissing, Pennsylvania. But little did she know, this move would be the first note in her symphony of a career. Taylor's love for singing was already budding, and she soon began performing at local events and venues all around the state of Pennsylvania. She even wrote her very first song, "Lucky You", while living there! It was during this time that she first heard of the legendary "Music City" aka Nashville, and her dream of moving there to take her music to new heights began to blossom.

Fun Facts!

- She spent her summers at a beach, Stone Harbor house on the Jersey Shore.
- At just 10 years old, Taylor was already entertaining crowds at local bashes, concerts, and fairs.
- She was really good at poetry! In fifth grade, she won a national competition with her poem, "Monster in My Closet."
- As if that wasn't impressive enough, at just 11 years old, Taylor sang the Star-Spangled Banner at a 76ers game. with thousands of people attending... watch out world, here comes Taylor!

I never want to change so much that people can't recogonize me."
-Taylor Swift

What makes you unique and how you've remained true to yourself despite changes in your life.

The Bright Lights

When Taylor Swift lived in Wyomissing, she had a lot of fun doing the things she loved. She started acting in a theater group. Imagine standing on stage with bright lights shining on you and acting out stories. It was here that she learned the art of performance. She also found she loved to sing karaoke. She would hold a microphone, the music would start, and she would sing her heart out, imagining she was one of the stars on the radio. All of this acting and singing wasn't just fun and games, it helped her learn to perform with confidence and sparkle - something she is pretty famous for now! So every time you do something like play pretend or sing a favorite tune, you can remember this is something she did when she was younger, and who knows, maybe you could be practicing to be a star too!

Fun Facts!

- Brace yourself for this one: Taylor's first song, the legendary "Lucky You," was penned when she was a mere 12 years old.
- As a student of Wyomissing Area Junior/Senior High, Taylor's love for singing and acting bloomed in the choir and theatre programs.
- The Berks Youth Theatre Academy Productions was her home stage, where she dazzled audiences with her performance skills.
- But wait, there's more! Taylor's acting coach even went the extra mile and rented a karaoke space for her at a local mall. The rest, as they say, is history!

"We are too busy dancing to get knocked on
our feet."
-Taylor Swift

Create a page with swirling patterns and music notes to represent an active life filled with joy and movement.

MORE FUN FACTS

- Her cat is named Meredith Grey, after a character from "Grey's Anatomy."
- Taylor likes to include secret messages in her album liner notes.
- In 2012, she lent her voice to the character Audrey in the animated film "The Lorax."
- Taylor has been in the public eye for her relationships with celebrities like Joe Jonas, Jake Gyllenhaal, and Tom Hiddleston.
- At the time it was performed, the "Reputation" Stadium Tour was the highest-grossing tour in US history.

MORE FUN FACTS

- Her album "Fearless" includes her first Billboard Hot 100 number one hit, "Love Story."
- "Speak Now" (2010), her third album, was completely self-written.
- She made her acting debut in the 2010 movie "Valentine's Day."
- In its first week in the US, "Speak Now" sold over a million copies.
- Taylor Swift has created songs for every letter of the alphabet, except Q and X.

HOW SWIFTY ARE YOU?

1. Where was Taylor Swift born?
   A) Reading, Pennsylvania
   B) New York City, New York
   C) Los Angeles, California
   D) Chicago, Illinois

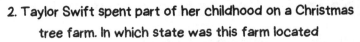

2. Taylor Swift spent part of her childhood on a Christmas tree farm. In which state was this farm located
   A) Texas
   B) Tennessee
   C) Pennsylvania
   D) North Carolina

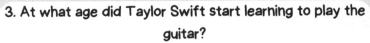

3. At what age did Taylor Swift start learning to play the guitar?
   A) 5 years old
   B) 10 years old
   C) 13 years old
   D) 16 years old

21

Answers on page 83

4. What was the name of Taylor Swift's first horse, which she received as a Christmas gift when she was 9 years old?

A) Buttercup

B) Cinnamon

C) Sparkle

D) Midnight

5. During her childhood, Taylor Swift often visited her grandmother's house, where she developed her interest in music. What musical instrument did her grandmother play?

A) Violin

B) Piano

C) Guitar

D) Banjo

6. Taylor Swift attended a private school for some part of her childhood. What was the name of this school?

A) Henderson High School

B) West Beverly High School

C) Wyndcroft School

D) Central High School

7. In her early teenage years, Taylor Swift performed at local venues and festivals in her hometown. What genre of music did she primarily perform during this time?

A) Country

B) Hip-hop

C) Rock

Answers on page 83

the Second
Act

Nashville

Taylor's passion for singing grew stronger each day, and she was captivated by stories of country singers who made it big in Nashville, Tennessee. Despite her parents' initial reluctance to move, Taylor persisted and eventually convinced them to take a trip to Nashville for a holiday. With a backpack full of her songs and homemade CD covers featuring cute drawings and a note that read "Call me please," Taylor was ready for an adventure.

During their trip, Taylor and her mom visited every music venue they could find, where Taylor eagerly dropped off her CDs in hopes of getting a callback. Although no one contacted her at that time, her parents recognized Taylor's unwavering dedication to her dream. They knew that this was only the beginning of her musical journey, and nothing could stand in the way of her aspirations.

Fun Facts!

- A record executive once advised her to stop copying other songs and start recording her own. This feedback completely changed the trajectory of her career.
- After watching a Faith Hill documentary, Taylor was inspired to move to Nashville to pursue her dream of becoming a country music artist.
- Taylor's ancestry includes Scottish, English, German, Irish, Italian, and Welsh roots.
- Taylor won a local talent competition with her rendition of LeAnn Rimes' "Big Deal" and was allowed to perform as the opening act for Charlie Daniels at a Strausstown amphitheater.

Opportunity

Picture yourself as a 14-year-old Taylor Swift, writing your music with dreams of becoming a sensation. Suddenly, a major record label, RCA Records, shows interest in you and offers to help you reach your full potential. As a mentor, RCA works with Taylor to improve her singing abilities. However, there is a catch - the label wants her to wait until she turns 18 before releasing her first album. Taylor has a notebook filled with songs and is eager to share them with the world, but RCA's conditions don't align with her vision.

After much contemplation, Taylor decides to part ways with RCA Records. It's a daunting decision since they are a well-established company, but Taylor trusts her instincts when it comes to her music. She embarks on a solo journey, without a record deal, and hopes for the best. Taylor believes in herself and refuses to compromise her values.

Fun Facts!

- She had an original track featured on a Maybelline compilation album called "Chicks with Attitude."
- She made an appearance during the "Rising Stars" campaign at Abercrombie and Fitch.
- She initially moved to Hendersonville, Tennessee, before settling in Nashville.
- By the age of 15, she had already written over 200 of her own songs.

"I think fearless is having fears, but jumping anyway."
-Taylor Swift

Think about a time when you faced your fears head-on. What fears are you currently experiencing and how can you overcome them?

Persistence

Persistence is key and Taylor's story is a testament to that. Following her departure from RCA, she began playing music at the Bluebird Cafe, a local cafe. During one of her performances, Scott Borchetta, a music label executive who was in the process of creating his own label called Big Machine Records, noticed her exceptional talent. Impressed by her performance, he signed her on as a singer. Recognizing this as a great opportunity, Taylor's family moved to Nashville, with her father transferring to the Nashville office. This move allowed them to be at the center of the country music industry and make connections with the right people at the right time. Taylor's perseverance, determination, and self-belief were all instrumental in her journey to becoming the artist she is today.

Fun Facts!

- Before establishing his record label, Scott Borchetta worked at DreamWorks Records.
- During her time in Nashville, Taylor Swift collaborated with experienced songwriters like Liz Roe, who helped her create the song "Teardrops on My Guitar."
- Taylor was determined to finish school, so when she moved to Nashville, she enrolled in Aaron Academy, a private Christian high school that provided homeschooling options.
- At the age of 16, Taylor Swift released her first album, "Taylor Swift," in 2006.

Platinum

Imagine being a teenager and accomplishing something as incredible as Taylor Swift did when she released her first album, "Taylor Swift," at only 16 years old. It has since remained on the Billboard 200 chart for an impressive 277 consecutive weeks!

This album is more than just a collection of songs; it's a reflection of Taylor's heart and hard work woven into melodies that will linger in your head for days. Each track mirrors a chapter of Taylor's life, filled with stories of crushes, aspirations, and staying true to oneself despite naysayers. The hit "Teardrops on My Guitar" feels like confiding secrets to your closest friend.

The album is a testament to bravery, passion, and resilience. Taylor sings about heartbreak and picking herself up again, all while strumming her guitar and wearing a smile that says, "I'm going to conquer the world." The RCA missed out on what they had when they dismissed Taylor, believing that she was too young to launch her career. They were mistaken, as Taylor's star quality could not be denied!

Fun Facts!

- She wrote "Our Song" for her high-school talent show.
- In the first week of its release, Taylor's debut album sold 39,000 copies.
- Taylor's social media following on MySpace is often credited for helping her achieve fame.
- Her first album successfully blended country and pop music genres.

"People haven't always been there for me,
but music has."
-Taylor Swift

When Taylor moved to Nashville, not every record label was interested in signing her. However, she didn't give up and continued to pursue her dreams. Can you think of a time you didn't give up on your dreams?

MORE FUN FACTS

- As a child, Taylor's primary hobby was English horseback riding, and competed in horse shows.
- At just 12 years old, she wrote her first song, "Lucky You."
- Her first single, "Tim McGraw," was released in 2006.
- In the same year, her self-titled debut album "Taylor Swift" was released. She wrote or co-wrote all the tracks on the album.
- Her second album, "Fearless," was released in 2008 and won four Grammy Awards.

MORE FUN FACTS

- She considers the number 13 to be her lucky number.
- She has been featured eight times in Time's list of the 100 most influential people in the world.
- In 2019, she received the Artist of the Decade award at the American Music Awards.
- Taylor Swift has a tradition of incorporating Easter eggs or hidden messages into her music videos.
- She wrote a song called "Ronan" in memory of a young boy who passed away from cancer at the age of four.

HOW SWIFTY ARE YOU?

8. Taylor Swift's first album was released when she was how old?

A) 15

B) 16

C) 17

D) 18

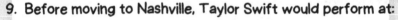

9. Before moving to Nashville, Taylor Swift would perform at:

A) Birthday parties

B) Karaoke contests

C) Shopping malls

D) All of the above

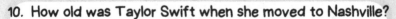

10. How old was Taylor Swift when she moved to Nashville?

A) 11

B) 13

C) 14

D) 16

39

Answers on page 83

11. What subject did Taylor Swift like most in school?
- A) Mathematics
- B) English
- C) History
- D) Science

12. Besides singing, what other talent did Taylor Swift showcase at the bluebird cafe that impressed Scott Borchetta?
- A) Dancing
- B) Songwriting
- C) Guitar playing
- D) Piano playing

13. What is the name of the songwriting method Taylor Swift uses, where she writes about her own life experiences?
- A) Fantasy writing
- B) Autobiographical writing
- C) Fictional writing
- D) Abstract writing

14. Which Taylor Swift song became a hit and talks about her personal experiences and feelings?
- A) "Shake It Off"
- B) "Teardrops on My Guitar"
- C) "Bad Blood"
- D) "Blank Space"

40

Answers on page 83

the Third
Act

Fearless

Let's talk about Taylor Swift's first three music albums – they're like four amazing chapters in her life, and each one is like flipping to a new part of her story.

1. "Taylor Swift" (2006): This is where it all begins! It's like Taylor's introduction, saying "Hi" to the world of music. She was just 16 – when this album came out. It has songs about school crushes and dreaming big, just like the stories you'd share with your friends. "Our Song" and "Teardrops on My Guitar" are like pages from her diary, turned into music that everyone loved.

2. "Fearless" (2008): Imagine your biggest, bravest dreams – that's "Fearless." It's like Taylor's victory lap in the music race. She sings about fairytales and real-life feelings, with songs like "Love Story" and "You Belong With Me." It's the album that won her a bunch of big music awards and made her super famous. She was telling the world that it's okay to be a little scared sometimes, as long as you're fearless at heart.

3. Speak Now" (2010): Now Taylor is growing up, and so is her music. "Speak Now" is like getting a whole album written just by Taylor, without any help – because that's actually what she did! This album has songs about saying sorry ("Back to December") and standing up for yourself ("Mean"). It's all about speaking up, and it feels like she's chatting right to us.

Fun Facts!

- The album "Fearless" earned four Academy Awards.
- Taylor Swift became the youngest person ever to win "Album of the Year."
- Her first three albums are known for their autobiographical storytelling, with songs based on her own life experiences.
- "Love Story" has sold over 18 million copies, making it one of the best-selling singles of all time.

44

Paint it "Red"

All right, so imagine you've been painting pictures with nothing but blue and green. Then one day, you decide to splash in some bright reds, yellows, and purples. That's kind of what Taylor Swift did with her album called "Red."

Before "Red," Taylor was like the queen of country music. She wrote songs that were like stories, and they had a special country twang. But with "Red," Taylor started to use different sounds that weren't just country. She added pop music to her paint palette.

"Red" has some of her famous country vibes, but it also has catchy beats and rhythms that make you want to jump up and dance. Songs like "We Are Never Ever Getting Back Together" were different from what she'd done before. They were super popular all over the world, and even people who didn't listen to country music started to sing along.

This change was really good for Taylor's career because it meant that more people could enjoy her music. By trying something new, Taylor showed everyone that she could sing different types of songs and still sound amazing.

So, "Red" helped Taylor not just to keep her old fans, but to make a lot of new ones too. She was able to bridge gaps between different people and connect them in ways that no one had ever been able to do before. Now country and Pop fans are united with the same love of the same songs, and the same love of the same person - Taylor Swift.

Fun Facts!

- The song "We Are Never Ever Getting Back Together" was the first one to make it to the Billboard Hot 100.
- Taylor was 22 years old at the time of the album's release.
- Taylor is well-known for being a "Bridge Builder," as she has successfully built bridges between various music groups uniting people.
- On the "Red" album, Taylor collaborated with several artists including Ed Sheeran and Gary Lightbody from Snow Patrol.

"The only way you can sustain a permanent change is to create a new way of thinking, acting, and being."
-Taylor Swift

Taylor underwent significant changes, leading to personal growth. Share one thing you would like to change in your life and how you plan to achieve it.

Reputation

In 2017 Taylor released her 6th album "Reputation. and it was like nothing we'd ever heard from her before.
"Reputation" had Taylor showing a tougher and more powerful side of her. It's like she said, "I'm ready to take on the world!" The first song, "Look What You Made Me Do," had a beat that made everyone sit up and listen. The music video was like a movie with Taylor playing all these different characters, even zombies!

The whole album was like a storybook filled with songs about battles she had won, how it feels when people don't understand you, and how sometimes, the world can be a little tough on you when you're famous. But it also had sweet songs about falling in love and finding happiness in the middle of all the craziness.

When "Reputation" came out, everyone everywhere was talking about it. It was number 1 on the Billboard 200 charts and over 1 million people bought it in the first week alone. Taylor even went on a giant tour, filling up huge stadiums with fans who came to dance and sing along.

"Reputation" was Taylor's way of telling her side of the story, with all the noise around her turned into powerful music. She showed all of us that no matter what, you can rise above and rock out, just like she does.

Fun Facts!

- The "Reputation" tour was a smashing success, becoming the highest-grossing tour in US history.
- After releasing "Reputation," Taylor Swift cleared out her old posts on Facebook and replaced them with a hissing snake image.
- In one of her music videos, Taylor included an image of a tombstone with the words "Here lies Taylor's reputation."
- Taylor Swift's "Reputation" album showcased a blend of electronic and pop music, proving her versatility once again!

Folklore

Taylor released her 8th album "Folklore" in 2020. It is full of songs that feel like fairy tales and deep thoughts all woven together. Taylor tells stories not just from her own life but also from different characters she imagined. It's like opening a book of short stories set to music. The songs touch on lost love, are whimsical, and have introspection, with haunting melodies that stick with you. The album includes songs like "Cardigan," "August," and "Betty," which quickly became fan favorites.

Just when fans thought Taylor had shared all she could for the year, she surprised everyone again in December 2020 with "Evermore," her ninth studio album. Think of "Evermore" as "Folklore's" mysterious sister; it continues the same indie-folk vibe but dives even deeper into the storytelling. It's like Taylor was painting with darker shades of the same color palette she used for "Folklore."

With "Evermore," Taylor explores new narratives and intricate emotions even further. The songs on this album feel like wandering through a misty forest of feelings and experiences. Tracks like "Willow," "No Body, No Crime," and "Ivy" showcase Taylor's knack for creating vivid, narrative lyrics that can transport you to other places and times.

These albums were a huge hit, both critically acclaimed and loved by fans, showing that Taylor can reinvent her music and storytelling time and again.

Fun Facts!

- "Evermore" was released five months after "Folklore."
- Both "Folklore" and "Evermore" belong to the Cottagecore genre, which captures the essence of serene and comfortable forests and surroundings.
- Taylor Swift won the Album of the Year award for "Folklore" at the 63rd Grammy Awards.
- Both albums were surprise releases with no promotion on social media or single releases. "Evermore" was announced just a few days before its release.

"You are not the Opinion of someone who doesn't know you."
-Taylor Swift

Taylor struggled with rumors and other people talking behind her back and learned to rise above it. Can you think of a time when you felt judged and how you overcame it?

MORE FUN FACTS

- Swift's "Speak Now" album was entirely recorded using live instruments.
- She owns not one, but two Dassault private jets.
- Her Rhode Island estate is famous for hosting her star-studded Fourth of July parties.
- Swift has a passion for vintage items and is an avid antique collector.
- Apart from her music, she is also known for baking delicious cookies and treats for her friends and colleagues.
- Last but not least, Swift has earned a star on the iconic Hollywood Walk of Fame.

MORE FUN FACTS

- She has starred in several movies, such as "The Giver" and "Cats."
- Taylor has received an honorary doctorate from Berklee College of Music.
- Her debut single, "Tim McGraw," came out in 2006.
- The music video for Swift's song "The Story of Us" was filmed in the library of Vanderbilt University.
- Taylor has appeared as a mentor on the popular TV show "The Voice," guiding aspiring singers.
- Swift made history as the first woman to receive the Album of the Year Grammy twice for her solo recordings.

15. How long did it take Taylor Swift to write Tim McGraw?
    A) 15 hours
    B) 15 minutes
    C) 15 days
    D) 15 years

16. Which of these musicians did NOT collaborate with Taylor Swift on "Folklore" and "Evermore"?
    A) Aaron Dessner
    B) Jack Antonoff
    C) Justin Bieber
    D) Justin Vernon

17. What is the title of the Disney film where Taylor Swift performed and discussed songs from "Folklore"
    A) "Folklore: The Movie"
    B) "Folklore: Taylor's Version"
    C) "Folklore: The Long Pond Studio Sessions"
    D) "Folklore: The Untold Stories"

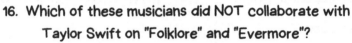

Answers on page 83

18. What was the lead single from "Folklore"?
   A) "Cardigan"
   B) "Willow"
   C) "Exile"
   D) "Betty"

19. What color is predominantly featured on the cover of "Evermore"?
   A) Blue
   B) Red
   C) Green
   D) Yellow

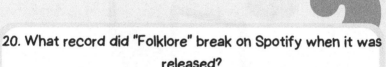

20. What record did "Folklore" break on Spotify when it was released?
   A) Most first-day streams for a pop album
   B) Most first-day album streams by a female artist
   C) Longest album to stay at number one
   D) Most songs in the top 10 at the same time

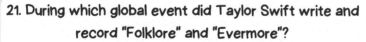

21. During which global event did Taylor Swift write and record "Folklore" and "Evermore"?
   A) The Olympics
   B) The FIFA World Cup
   C) The COVID-19 pandemic
   D) The Super Bowl

Answers on page 83

the Fourth
Act

Friend Love

Taylor Swift is of course artistic and talented but there is even more to her than that, what are her values? One of them is her close-knit friends. Taylor Swift is known for having a close circle of friends, and she's often seen hanging out with them, just like you might with your buddies. Her friends include people she's met in different parts of her life, like school, her music career, and even other famous people she's met at events.

She's super supportive of her friends and is known for throwing awesome parties for them, like her famous Fourth of July parties. She also writes songs about them sometimes, and they even show up in her music videos, like in "Bad Blood," which was like a big party where all her friends acted as characters in the video.

Taylor and her friends stand up for each other too. If one of them has a problem or is feeling down, she's there to help out. And even though she's super famous, she still finds time to bake cookies, celebrate birthdays, and do normal friend stuff.

But like everyone, she's had ups and downs with friends. Sometimes she's not as close with someone as she used to be, which is pretty normal because friendships can change. But the coolest part is, that Taylor often talks about how important her girlfriends are and how much she loves having strong women around her. They're like a squad of besties who have a lot of fun, support each other, and make great memories together!

Fun Facts!

- Taylor Swift has a group of friends that some refer to as themselves as the "celebrity squad," which includes Selena Gomez, Emma Stone, and Ed Sheeran. She often attends their parties, premieres, and music video shoots.
- Taylor's friendships are so important to her that she has even written songs about them. For example, "Fifteen" was written for her high school friend Abigail Anderson, and she has been known to include details about her friends' life events in her music.
- Taylor has been a part of many of her friends' significant life events. She was a bridesmaid for Abigail and attended three of her friends' baby showers.

Family love

Taylor Swift's family holds a special place in her heart, and she believes they are a crucial part of her life. Her mom and dad helped her get started with her music, and her brother, Austin, has also been a part of her journey – starring in some of her music videos. Taylor has written many songs about her family, including "The Best Day," which captures all the fun times she had with her mom. She also wrote a poignant song when her mom fell ill, as a way to express her love and support.

Taylor always makes sure to thank her family during awards ceremonies or other significant events, recognizing the role they've played in her success. She occasionally brings them along to big events, and their support for each other is evident. Despite her fame, Taylor respects her family's privacy and ensures that they can live a normal life. She keeps some things just for them, away from the public's attention. Taylor's family is truly a team, and they cheer each other on, no matter what.

Fun Facts!

- Her brother Austin made an appearance in the music video for "I Don't Want to Live Forever."
- The song "Soon You'll Get Better" was written about her mother's battle with cancer in 2015. It's a very personal song for Taylor, and she avoids performing it because she knows she'll become emotional.
- Taylor often credits her family for keeping her grounded and regularly mentions them during interviews and speeches.
- Both "Evermore" and "Folklore" were surprise releases without any pre-release singles or social media announcements. "Evermore" was announced just a few days before its release.

"My Friends are the kind of people who have brought me so much light in my life, so much joy and in some cases a reality check and in some cases motivation."
-Taylor Swift

Taylor values the grounding effect of close friends and family. What do you value in yours and how do you stay true to them?

Giving Back

Taylor Swift has a big heart when it comes to giving back. Known for her generosity, she's made headlines multiple times for her charitable acts. She's donated millions of dollars to causes like education, disaster relief, and the LGBTQ+ community. For example, she's given money to schools to help improve education and even donated to the Tennessee flood relief to help people whose homes were destroyed by natural disasters. Taylor also stands up for what she believes in, like when she made a big donation to support LGBTQ+ rights. She doesn't just give money; she also spends time visiting sick kids in hospitals, making their day a little brighter with her music and smile. It's clear that for Taylor, being charitable is not just about writing checks; it's about making a real difference in people's lives and using her spotlight to shine a light on important issues.

Fun Facts!

- Taylor learned how to play guitar on a 12-string guitar instead of a six-string (the normal guitar).
- She wrote a book at the age of 14 called "A Girl Named Girl." It was actually about a family that wanted a son but instead had a daughter.
- She sang in her local high school talent show and won with the song "Our Song" which she later had in one of her albums.
- Taylor gave her first "gold record" to a singer on Rascall Flatts-Eric Church, as a way to say "thank you."

68

Fan love

Taylor Swift's relationship with her fans, affectionately known as "Swifties," is more than just appreciation; it's a heartfelt connection that she nurtures with genuine care and affection. Taylor acknowledges her fans' role in her success and goes above and beyond to make them feel valued. She's known for personal gestures like sending surprise holiday gifts, handwritten notes, and even responding to fans' social media posts and life events.

This unique bond is also celebrated in her frequent interactions with fans during concerts, meet-and-greets, and impromptu gatherings. Her surprise "Secret Sessions" before album releases—where she invites fans to listen to her new music before it's public—are legendary, creating an inclusive, family-like atmosphere.

Taylor actively listens to their stories and often reaches out with support during their tough times. Be it offering financial assistance for education, giving advice on love and heartbreak, or comforting fans through personal crises, Taylor's compassion is always evident. She's also been known to engage in acts of kindness, like visiting fans in the hospital or inviting them backstage for a more personal meet-up. For Taylor, fans are not just spectators in her journey; they're an integral part of her narrative, and she treats them with the same enthusiasm and respect they show her, fostering a mutual love that is rare and sincere in the world of celebrity.

Fun Facts!

- Before the release of her albums, Taylor hosts "secret sessions" to give her fans an exclusive listening party at her house.
- Swiftmas: During the holiday season, she sends personalized gifts to her fans.
- In her music video "Me", Taylor features a snake that transforms into a butterfly, which many believe symbolizes her growing and changing relationship with her fans.
- Amid the COVID-19 pandemic, Taylor has assisted fans who were experiencing financial difficulties by sending them donations.

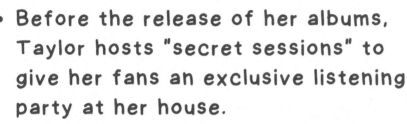

"No matter what happens in life, be good to people. Being good to people is a wonderful legacy to leave behind."
-Taylor Swift

Taylor is dedicated to making a positive impact on her fans' lives. What can you do to positively influence others?

Complete the lyrics

1. "And all the pieces fall, right into place. Getting caught up in a moment, lipstick on your face..."
   - A) So it goes...
   - B) I'm yours to keep
   - C) I'm yours to lose
   - D) Every single day

2. "Cause baby now we got bad blood, you know it used to be mad love..."
   - A) So take a look what you've done
   - B) But now we're not even friends
   - C) Cause baby now we got problems
   - D) So take a look what I've done

3. "And I can't help but to think of it's best you went away..."
   - A) I hope you remember today is never too late
   - B) But what about our future plans?
   - C) I hope you remember that today is never too late
   - D) But what happens when the summer fades away?

73

Answers on page 84

4. "I'm so sick of running as fast as I can, wondering if I'd get there quicker if I was a man..."
- A) And I'm so sick of them coming at me again
- B) Would it be enough?
- C) Wondering if I'd get there quicker if I was a man
- D) And I'm so tired of pretending

5. "He said the way my blue eyes shined, put those Georgia stars to shame that night..."
- A) I said, that's a lie
- B) I said, that's alright
- C) I said, that's a sight
- D) I said, just keep on shining

6. "You take me home, just to break me like a promise. So casually cruel in the name of being honest..."
- A) I'm a crumpled-up piece of paper lying here
- B) I'm scattered around like pieces on the floor
- C) I'm shattered like a window pane
- D) I'm crushed under the weight of your words

7. "I don't know about you, but I'm feeling 22. Everything will be alright if..."
- A) You keep me next to you
- B) You just keep dancing like we're 22
- C) We just keep dancing like we're 22
- D) We stay up all night

74

Answers on page 83

8. "Say you'll remember me, standing in a nice dress, staring at the sunset, babe..."
- A) Red lips and rosy cheeks
- B) Barefoot in the grass
- C) With that old sweet smile
- D) Lipstick marks on your coffee cup

9. "I don't wanna live forever, 'cause I know I'll be living in vain..."
- A) And I don't wanna fit wherever
- B) And I don't want to keep on wishing
- C) And I don't want you to go
- D) And I can't get you out of my brain

10. "We are never ever getting back together, we..."
- A) Are never ever getting back together
- B) Said never say never
- C) Are done forever
- D) Said goodbye forever

Answers on page 84

"I think the perfection of love is that it is not perfect."
-Taylor Swift

76

77

the Final
Act

The Future

We don't know exactly what could be in Taylor's future, but one thing is for certain, it will be something amazing! She will probably re-imagine her music once again and build more bridges. She may decide to start acting more. I am certain she will continue to keep helping others whether that is friends, family, fans, causes, or just someone in need. She may become a businesswoman and create a clothing line (wouldn't that be amazing!). One thing is for certain whatever it may be it will certainly make the world a better place because that is what she does best: reinvent, reimagine, redesign, and improve everything around her.

Regardless of what she chooses to pursue, Taylor's fans are eagerly anticipating her next moves.

What can you imagine for your future? How can your tomorrow be a better today?

_____
_____
_____
_____
_____
_____
_____
_____
_____
_____
_____
_____
_____
_____
_____
_____
_____
_____
_____
_____
_____
_____
_____

Music video matchup

Directions: Below is a list of performers featured in Taylor Swift's music videos. Match the performer with the character they portrayed in the video. Write the letter of the correct character next to the performer's name.*

Performers:

1. Taylor Swift
2. Ed Sheeran
3. Sean O'Pry
4. Zendaya
5. Hayley Williams
6. Tyler Hilton
7. Dominic Sherwood
8. Kendrick Lamar
9. Riley Keough
10. Justin Sandy

Answers on page 83

Music video matchup

Characters:

A. The jealous ex-girlfriend ("We Are Never Ever Getting Back Together")

B. The romantic love interest ("Style")

C. The roguish groom ("Speak Now")

D. The intense love interest ("End Game")

E. Taylor's on-screen partner in a toxic relationship ("Blank Space")

F. The antagonist in an epic battle ("Bad Blood")

G. The leading man in a story of love and heartbreak ("Wildest Dreams")

H. The leader of a rival squad ("Bad Blood")

I. The other woman ("I Knew You Were Trouble")

J. The high school sweetheart ("You Belong With Me")

Answers on page 83

How Swifty Are you?

1. **A**
2. **C**
3. **B**
4. **A**
5. **D**
6. **C**
7. **A**
8. **B**
9. **D**
10. **C**
11. **B**
12. **B**
13. **B**
14. **B**
15. **B**
16. **C**
17. **C**
18. **A**
19. **C**
20. **B**
21. **C**

Complete the Lyrics: (page 73/74)

1. A) so it goes
2. A) so take a look what you've done
3. C I hope you remember that day is never too late
4. A) And I'm so sick of them coming at me again
5. B) I said, that's alright
6. A) I'm a crumpled-up piece of paper lying here
7. A) You keep me next to you
8. A) Red lips and rosy cheeks
9. D) And I can't get you out of my brai
10. A) Are never ever getting back together

Music Video Matchup (page 81/82)

1. Taylor Swift - E. Taylor's on-screen partner in a toxic relationship ("Blank Space")
2.. Ed Sheeran - D. The intense love interest ("End Game")
3. Sean O'Pry - G. The leading man in a story of love and heartbreak ("Wildest Dreams")
4. Zendaya - H. The leader of a rival squad ("Bad Blood")
5. Hayley Williams - F. The antagonist in an epic battle ("Bad Blood")
6. Tyler Hilton - C. The roguish groom ("Speak Now")
7. Dominic Sherwood - B. The romantic love interest ("Style")
8. Kendrick Lamar - F. The antagonist in an epic battle ("Bad Blood")
9. Riley Keough - A. The jealous ex-girlfriend ("We Are Never Ever Getting Back Together")
10. Justin Sandy - J. The high school sweetheart ("You Belong With Me")

Shine on bright Star!

I believe one important lesson we can learn from Taylor is that if you set your mind and heart to it, you can achieve anything. Although you may be small at the moment your dreams have the power to take you to great heights, and when the time comes, you will shine brightly!

How can you bring out the best in yourself
and shine like a star?

_____
_____
_____
_____
_____
_____
_____
_____
_____
_____
_____
_____
_____
_____
_____
_____
_____
_____
_____

Made in the USA
Middletown, DE
19 December 2023